LET'S TAKE
THE LONG WAY

POEMS, PRAYERS &
PROMISES

ELISSA COBB

ISBN: 978-1-935874-32-4

SATYA

HOUSE

Poems are dear creatures that seem to climb out of my soul and perch near the back door of my mind patiently waiting for me to let them in. They always begin with just a few words that have a certain rhythmic urgency. They repeat their simple phrases inside me until I have no choice but to sit down and put pen to paper. Then they run down my arm and flow through the ink to write themselves.

Some of these particular poems came during meditations and yoga practices. Some came during sleep. And some I found along the road of everyday experiences.

Thank you for picking up this book, and for reading what wanted to be written.

To all those wanderers whose faithful feet are well worn, whose minds are weary from wondering, and whose hearts still get up every morning and sing songs of praise, no matter what.

Thank you, Martin Prechtel, for the phrase "My grief becomes my beauty," and the root essences for the poem, Kind-Hearted Mystery, both of which have been a balm to my heart since I heard these words from you.

CONTENTS

THE WAY IN

Make beautiful the way in . . .
Clear the overgrowth from the gate.
Break free and oil the rusted hinges.
And set about widening the narrowed path.

Make beautiful the way in . . .
Pull the tenacious weeds.
Dig out the invasive species.
Loosen the soil and turn the worms.
And wear the scent of dirt as a rare essential oil.

Make beautiful the way in . . .
Trim back the brambled tentacles of roses.
Let them tear your old skin . . .
Just a little . . .
A tattoo . . . a small rite of passage . . .

Make beautiful the way in.
Make space for things longing to bloom.
Catch your breath with their beauty.
Let them cause you to sit down
And write poems.

Make beautiful the way in.
Peer beneath rocks.
Scatter spiders and beetles.
Be startled by handsome snakes.
Dance and twirl and hum with the winged things.

Make beautiful the way in.
Prop up the drooping peonies
Full of the damp weight of life.
Pile the restless memories of plants in wheelbarrows
And escort them graciously to the compost heap.

Finally, sweep clean the porch steps.
Set right the statues and water the fountains.
Then sit upon the sweet veranda of your heart,
Sip iced tea with mint,
And dream your next dream.

BALM

All I ever really need to do
To sooth myself
In the face of change
Is wait a minute,
And another,
And another,
Until I forget that I have been waiting.

Then I notice
That something in me
Has naturally shifted.
If not a lot,
Then, at least,
A little,
And I am ready to take a bite . . .
A taste of what is new . . . now . . .

What a blessing!
That,
As my thoughts wander away from the hard moment
And curl up under the bittersweet vines,
My soul comes home
And airs out the house . . .
Turns the porch light back on
So I can find my way back again,
Less afraid . . .
And somehow improved.

Could it be that change,
Received smaller doses,
Digested a little at a time
Can actually be a balm?
To wounds infected
By trying to stay the same?

PUZZLE

This human life is,
Indeed,
A puzzle,
And I don't recall
The image on the package . . .
The finished picture
Of who I am to be.

I came here with the corner pieces . . .
My beginnings . . .
Since then
Every turn,
Each moment,
Looking for the borders.
A piece here . . .
A piece there.

Sometimes I find oddly shaped ones
That fit perfectly into place.
Or a piece that I hold onto
For a while,
My fingers hovering,
Searching for the hopeful spot.
But then I have to set it aside
On the edge of the table,
No clear place to put it
Yet.

On occasion,
I receive a small hand-made gift bag
Containing a few treasured pieces
Long missing . . .
Lost . . .
As if dropped under the rug somewhere.
And now and then
Some other strange grouping
That leads me to a whole new area
Of my puzzle.
My focus shifting,
The bigger picture gracefully unfolding.

Some pieces are given when I pray,
Or when I remember to listen.
But most come unexpectedly.
Some even arrive unwanted,
And some, withheld to test my patience.

There are pieces that arrive
Just in the nick of time!
Others are apparently on backorder . . .
Or delivered to a seemingly incorrect address.
And then there are times
When pieces of my puzzle
Aren't at all what I ordered from the catalog.
No returns or exchanges.

Somehow, though,
Everything . . .
All the individual pieces fit together
Eventually . . .
Always . . .
Edge-to-edge,
Through fumbling insight.

And I wonder if it isn't better
To live with the mystery
Of that yet unknown,
Incomplete illustration
Of the whole completed me.

To dance with the pieces . . .
To throw them up in the air
And see where they'll land,
Learning to trust
The process of becoming.

I am not afraid
of this tear...

THIS TEAR

I AM NOT AFRAID OF THIS TEAR.
The one that just escaped the cup of my eye
And is, even now,
Winding its patient way down my flushed cheek
Telling a story that requires no explanation
Or Translation,
Despite questioning looks and curiosities.

I am NOT afraid of this tear
That has no desire to hide from sight . . .
That makes no apologies for its being . . .
That knows no fear of its own . . .
No embarrassment . . .
No vulnerability.

I AM not afraid of this tear.
This small warm drop of salt water
That unknowingly casts the reflections
Of human experience
And primes the internal well of witnesses.

I am not AFRAID of this tear,
Which contains truth and authenticity . . .
And honestly betrays my boundaries
Creating both discomfort
And relief.

I am not afraid of this tear.
So why,
In this moment of its tumbling glory,
Do I wipe it away?

The precipice of sameness...

LEVERAGE

When Life
Becomes a lever
Wanting to pry me loose
From my stuck spot,
Wanting to dig the ground out from underneath
My roots,
Wanting to roll my stone away
Over the precipice
Of sameness . . .

The teacher in me
Arises in me
And calls me —
Commands me —
To sit at my own feet
And listen patiently
To the truth that will give me strength
To step back
And join Life
In my uprooting.

TETHER

Did I agree to this —
This tether bound so tightly around my wrist —
Back a long time ago?

I can't remember.
If I did,
I don't think I knew it would turn out this tight.

You see how it cuts into my flesh
Here?
It bleeds just a little every day.

Perhaps I thought it would wear through
By now.
How long has it been?

You see, it keeps me from moving past the far edge of this circle,
Outside of the well-packed ring
Worn smooth from going round and round.

Did we make it out of fear —
This tether —
That keeps me tied inside the boundary of us?

The line is taut.
My body aches . . . leans out, my feet digging in
Pulling away as far as I can.

You stand at the center flying me like a kite,
Smiling at the tug of my wind,
Thinking "That's far enough . . ."

Why don't I just cut this string —
This bloody, annoying cord of attachment
That no longer makes sense?

Do you hear me?
Look at what you hold in your hands.
The other end is me.

I wonder . . .
How hard will you land
When I decide to let go?

PRUNING

Fear is a seed that plants itself.
It needs not tilled ground
Nor human hand
To thrive . . .
No shallow, neat furrows dug,
Finger-deep . . .
No inch by inch,
No row by row.

Fear is an invasive species,
Blown in on the breezes of circumstance
Like milkweed or dandelion,
Carried on clear water like cattail pollen,
Or whispered into the long root of my spine.

At its heart,
Fear is kind.
It seeks to bloom bright with promises,
Wanting to keep me safe,
While believing I am not,
And hidden,
Believing I am vulnerable.

But fear grows like wild vines
Crowding out
Joy and laughter,
Adventure and possibility.
It covers up dreams and pleasure,
And wishes and chances,
As if they were long-abandoned temples.

The trick is to prune fear back
Gently . . .
At the right time and places . . .
Just barely behind its new buds,
So as not to kill it,
But to tend to it.

A FALSE FEELING

There is no such thing as disconnection.
It is an imaginary state of being.
A false feeling.
A pretend invention based on a crumbling foundation.
A dark, lonely tent
Pitched in the wind of Truth.

Self-separation
Is the tedious work
Of lovable fools,
And I count myself among them!

Solitude? Yes.
Uniqueness? Yes.
Differentiation? Yes.
Disconnection? Impossible.

Wisdom waits behind exhaustion
To catch us where we fall
From our repeated attempts
To set ourselves apart.

We land, not hard,
But in the ever-buoyant web of joyful connection
That was,
For a while,
Invisible.

What is the
range of motion
of my heart?

THE ARMS OF MY HEART

What is the range of motion of my heart?
What informs my choice to love or not love?

Give it or receive it?
Open it or close it off?
Extend it or withdraw it?

What un-meetable standards have I set
That unevenly define the degree to which I love?

To what extent do I allow my heart to come out and play . . .
To leap and dance and whisper in God's ear
The old song all hearts remember
And yearn to hear again, and again?

How long are the arms of my heart?
How much or how many do they softly hold?
Who or what lies within or beyond my heart's presumed
capacity?

I think, perhaps . . .
Maybe . . .
Probably . . .
Not loving the unlovable creates in me
Suffering undeserved.

UNRAKED

I am,
At certain times,
A yard unraked . . .
Compressed under a mat
Of damp color,
The decay of my old stories
Warming some new chapter
Beneath their compost.

Some paragraphs,
Though,
Having dehydrated . . .
Lost their juices . . .
Are loosely tossed about
By gusts of exciting uncertainty,
To be,
Eventually,
Blown down the street by a cleansing wind
Never to be seen again.

I consciously build piles of the most brilliant pages —
Like leaves —
To joyfully tumble into . . .
Roll around in . . .
Appreciate one more time
Before pulling them
To the shoulder of the road
Where,
Once ignited,
They blaze and sizzle,
Reaching back to me
With a sugar-sweet
Pungent smoke
That I recognize
As my own scent.

THE PERSPECTIVE
OF THE SLEEVE

My heart
Is back on my sleeve
Where it belongs,
Relieved in its vulnerability.

I feel it there.
Becoming more comfortably perched
Everyday,
Finding its balance.

For a time
I had hidden it
Several layers deeper
Where I thought it would be safer.
Where I thought
It needed to be
For its own good,
For protection.

Not trusting its capacity
To balance pain with pleasure,
Grief with joy,
Betrayal with forgiveness.

Somehow I remembered
To allow my patient heart
The gracious dignity
Of all experience
And from the perspective of the sleeve
Rediscovered my strength.

TOTAL RECALL

It seems I had adapted too well
To not being myself.
Well past knowing who I truly was
Most of the time.
It happened so slowly . . .
So quietly . . . that I fooled myself.
Although,
Looking back,
There were signs . . .

Saying "yes" on top of a trembling "no."
Or believing in something fiercely,
While feeling a part of my heart
Longing to pull the thread
That would unravel
Everything I used to "know."

Then came a perfect storm
Of changes in rapid fire succession,
And my grasping to hold onto something —
Anything —
To keep from drowning in uncertainties and blatant shocks.
My heart pleaded with me to shift my focus
From pain to pleasure . . .
A reprieve.

I didn't know how to do that then.
Had I ever really done that?
So many parts of me insisting on doubting that change
Had finished its rounds with me for now,
Which, of course, it never does . . .
I pretended to hope, fully expecting the other shoe to drop,
Which, of course, it always does . . .

I became worn away by change.
Polished by the flow of exhaustion,
Carved deep by suffering . . .
By my choice to suffer . . .
Being, after all, the source of my stress,
If not the cause . . .

Those educators in the form of change
Pushed me in a dimly lit direction
In an accelerated, slow motion way.
Over the edge of staying the same,
Falling into total recall
Of myself, my soul,
My truth.

Perhaps,
Just maybe,
Pleasure has been patient enough to wait for me
To land.

IN WINTER

In winter,
Having given up their leaves,
Trees unveil their secrets.
Those things hidden for quite some time
In green seclusion:
　Hornet homes
　　Squirrel baskets
　　　Bird nests
　　　　Broken limbs
　　　　Burls
And other unusual growths.
　Woodpecker holes
　　Tattered kites
And hungry, keen-eyed raptors.
　Playful crows
　　Tattered leaves
　　　Tenacious vines.

They stand there —
The trees —
On the other side
Of the relief of exposure,
Resting peacefully,
Rooting deeper,
Patiently juicing up with spring sap,
Titillated by the red quickening in their fingertips.

I stare at them,
Out the window
Of the back seat
Of this Subaru,
A kindred hider of secrets,
But more likely to remain a keeper of cover,
Less willing to be vulnerable,
Shying from truths,
Wary of the kind winds of change
That intend to somehow help me grow.

WRITING TODAY . . .

If I were going to write today,
I would write about how Spring almost forgot to come . . .
How everything stayed so cold and so wet
For so long
That we wondered if She had given up on us,
Having found some other more intriguing place to go.
How, daily, we peered hopefully
Beyond the brave tulips to the violet and trillium buds.
I might have written about this,
But I don't feel like writing today . . .

If I were going to write today,
I would compose some sort of symphony
Of joy remembered and pain forgotten,
Of rapturous gratitude and aching grief,
Of serrated separation and tentative relief,
Of attachment to how things were
And longing for how they could be.
I might have written about this,
But I don't feel like writing today . . .

If I were going to write today,
I would write about how Time,
Who was supposed to stand still
When you died,
Suddenly, overnight, turned hours into weeks,
Abandoning that moment when you let go
So you could go Home,
No longer bound by form,
Having figured out how to go to where Spring,
Perhaps,
Had hoped to follow,
Missing you as much as I did . . . do . . .
I might have written about all this, too,
But I don't feel like writing today.

LOVE

It is not enough to love.
Not enough to give it
Or receive it.

You must also,
Somehow,
Come to believe in it
As an entity
With it's own intentions.

Come to believe that Love
Has a life of it's own.
That it will always . . .
Does always . . .
Often in the quietest, most subtle,
Unexpected,
Even unnoticeable moments,
Find it's way back to you.

You must believe that Love
Somehow believes in you,
Too.
Whether it's evening shadows
Wrap silently around your shoulders,
Or whether it comes back
Like a bee sting to your heart,
Love forsakes no one
Forever.

PILGRIMAGE

What if we believed
That the reason for sleeping was this:
　　To return each night
　　To the open arms of Great Mystery?
　　To reconnect . . .
　　Tap back into energetic essence?

Our unique threads of consciousness
Weaving their way back
Into the enormous fabric
That we all belong to?

To be witnessed in our humanity
And reconfirmed as divine?
To be renewed, recharged, revamped . . .
Dusted, washed, shape-shifted . . .
Held, calmed, softened, integrated . . .
Sensed, seen, heard, felt . . .
Counseled, challenged, validated . . .
And drenched in understanding?

What if those first evening yawns
Were our ancestors calling us home
For a visit?
Drooping eyelids like chimes
To a silent circle of knowing?
Softening bodies' invitations
To temporarily step out of our jeweled forms?

How long, then,
Would we keep working late?
Staying up at night,
Keeping us from all of this possibility?
Would we still read just one more page?
Would we still hang on so tightly
To our human days?

Believing this . . .
(If we did . . .)
What rituals might prepare us
For such a blessed reunion?
For such a profound pilgrimage?
How would we ready our hearts?
Say our prayers?
Express our gratitude?

And what would we do . . .
How would we behave . . .
What would we change . . .
When we woke up in the morning,
Human again?

WEIGHTED

An Ant . . .
And not a big one,
One of those miniscule creatures,
Falsely insignificant,

Respectfully,
Because of its weighted importance,
Carries the thin bulk
Of a red, papery leaf,
Almost transparent,
And four times his size,
Like a sail on a tiny ship.
Tossed and tugged unpredictably
To and fro . . .
The skill of toting impossibility
With determination.

Not warrior-like.
More like a construction worker.
Skillfully adding part to part
To create an unknown,
Never before seen,
Yet genetically remembered
Whole thing.

These strange hopes and dreams of mine,
Like that torn corner of dry leaf . . .
Borne in my mandibles,
Over my back,
Across my shoulders,
Are weighted and uneven . . .
Tricky to balance with the day-to-day.

The ant, though,
As an example,
Tries and fails,
And tries and fails,
To carry his treasure
Intentionally . . . repeatedly
Over the edge of a concrete step
Miles high.

Again and again,
To that edge
He wanders, wonders, tries . . .
Until,
The best path found,
Clears the testing wall
To show me what is possible.

THE STONE, THE PEA AND THE THORN

What if,
No matter how far you walked,
The stone in your shoe would not dislodge?

What if,
No matter how much you tossed or turned,
The pea under your mattresses
Still kept you awake at night?

What if,
No matter how tall you stood,
The thorn in your side
Held fast?

What if
(And you know this is true)
The only way to walk,
Or sleep,
Or stand . . .
Was to stop everything
Long enough
To befriend . . .
To fully feel . . .
To stop fighting . . .
To get to know the true nature
And the profound dignity
Of the Stone . . .
The Pea . . .
And the Thorn?

THE LONG WAY
for Karen Hasskarl

Let's take the long way,
Even though the time grows short.
Let's make the most of it
Right now, while we can.

Let's take the long way,
And fool our wary hearts and churning minds,
Even though it's getting dusky
At the edges of the day.

Let's take the long way.
There may be comfort in the cooling moon,
A balm tucked into the soles of our tired shoes,
And something else
Not quite yet discerned to be revealed.

Let's take the long way.
Let's try the patience of Future,
And spend our last resources bribing Time.
Surely what is too soon to come
Will just have to wait.

TAKE HEART

Take heart.
The leaves are falling.
Fully, freely, finally falling.
Down, up, sideways, all ways,
Once again.

Rediscover.
We assumed that they would fall again
This year
Because they always do.
We hoped.
We anticipated.
And yet,
When the moment of falling comes,
We are always . . .
Somehow . . .
Caught off guard.

Pay attention.
Delight in the spiral dance
Of random transition.
Not being blown free
From the branch . . .
Not dying off . . .
Not leaving of their own accord.
But rather being set free
From their former attachments.

Heed the example.
Really, it is not to be missed.
This willingness
On the part of the trees
To no longer hold on
To the leaves that it loves.
To understand that otherwise
Things pile up,
Weight on weight,
Snow on branch,
Come winter.

Take note.
Even when leaves are the most glorious
In hue and scent . . .
The most worthy of coveting . . .
Likely to be stolen
By human hands
To be pressed in books and waxed paper.
Still they are allowed to fall.

Partake.
Live to tell the story
Of when you joined
The Letting Go Dance.
Of when you jumped for joy
In the leaves.
Of when you learned
That snow weighs easier
On clean branches.

MERCY

As when meeting the Buddha on the road,
When it comes time to kill
A certain part of myself
Out of mercy,
A mercy killing . . .
It can take a very long time, for it to die.

Peaceful starvation may be the best way,
Although it seems a long wait.

Strangulation, perhaps,
As another choice,
But this can be exhausting.

I'm not sure about drowning,
As these sort of parts refuse to remain submerged.

Yes . . . I think starvation is the most humane
And effective.

Just stop feeding it
Til it wanders off,
Or decides to stop eating at you
And withers away.

Remember though that it once served you well . . .
Was created for a reason
Worthy of some gratitude.

A painful process to be sure . . .
Difficult to be present to
Because the inner empathy steps forward
The care-giver part that has trouble with death with dignity.

Sit next to it.
Make peace with it.
Say "Good-bye,"
And sense the empty void it leaves behind
Without rushing in to fill it up.

SPARK

Have you a hidden spark?
Some gem inside kept secret?
A yearning that you keep quiet in a box
On a shelf
In your soul?
That thing that might make you, "you"?
That would change the size of the world
So that it would fit.

"Yes?"

Then, instead . . .
Seek the fire
That will incinerate
The compressed layers
Of all the old skins
You have shed so far.
Burn through the humus of your past.
Evaporate the overgrowth of self-limitations
Or self-destruction,
And ignite what's been waiting for so long . . .
What your raw heart has been yearning for.

Then, like the patient Sequoia,
Fearlessly let go that seed . . . that spark
Into the flame . . .
Into the tender, sore ground
Beneath you.
Revel in its vulnerable tenacity.
Feed it.
Bring it to life.
Pray over it.
Keep it visible . . . felt . . . no matter what.

Who knows how great
And surprising
It might become?

— Sequoia National Park

SHEDDING

I seem to have been walking around for some time now
Without my skin.
It was divinely removed
In great swaths,
And I was revealed, again . . .
Raw, sore, jagged and exposed.
Vulnerable, soft, not very well contained.
Self-conscious, oozing and dripping.
Attempting to not leave a trail.

But lately, some new skin is forming
In crazy quilt fashion . . .
Unpredictable, complicated, unfinished.
Delicate, hopeful, colorful, unique.

In its incompletion,
It feels awkward . . .
Loose-fitting and cumbersome,
Like pants with no drawstring . . .
Or a shirt with just one sleeve . . .
A shoe without laces . . .
Sloppy, fumbling, distracting.

It changes moment-by-moment,
Adjusting . . .
As if some familiar, patient hand
Is easing in some new piece of cloth
Across a tender internal plane,
Stitching it perfectly into place.
Drawing up an unseen,
Yet felt,
Thread,
That will inevitably . . . someday . . .
Be tugged at and unraveled once again
In favor of shedding.

THIS DAY

I will rise up to my light
Again this day,
Willing to be a fool for love,
For dreams,
And for this adventure
Called life.

I will meet myself this day
With open arms
On the dance floor
In my heart,
And twirl my skirts
To the music of my soul.

I will dust the shelves
Of my discontent,
And set out my collections
Of inspirations,
Precious memories,
And clear-eyed intentions.

I will receive each moment
As it comes,
Whether it strokes my sorrow
Into wakening,
Or teases my joy
Into singing.

Then,
At the end of this day,
I will rest like moss
On a turtle's back,
Float with myself
On a quiet pond of happiness,
And like my own company.

EXTENDED STAY AT
RUMI'S GUEST HOUSE

Rumi wrote about the Guest House,
But he forgot to mention the Extended Stay Option.

Apparently, there is some regulatory clause
That gives certain parts of us
An offer they just can't refuse:

"Participating innkeepers allow an indefinite stay
At half price
For any Behavior Patterns and Personal Beliefs that qualify."

"In order to qualify,
Above mentioned limitations must have been 'in effect'
For a documented minimum of 20 years . . .
Or more . . .
Show tangible proof of interference with relationships,
And be a card-carrying member of AAA,
(Always Absolutely Annoying)."

Okay . . . so . . . "Yes" . . .
Rumi,
In his melancholy wisdom,
Rightfully respected all guest behaviors and beliefs
As teachers,
Gurus to be well served
And honored for their time served.
But wouldn't it have been helpful
To have also been advised
To "read the small print" at the end of the contract?

"This offer may be good for infinity . . .
And beyond . . .
And while it cannot be used in addition to other discounts,
It can be applied continuously as needed
Provided no change in behavior occurs."

BOAT

I don't need a boat
To sail,
I don't need a plane to soar.
No need for wind
To be always at my back —
The Olde Irish Blessing . . .
No need to click the heels
Of ruby shoes
Three times
Like Dorothy.

The thing with wings —
The hope —
That perches in my soul
According to Emily Dickenson
Is enough to lift me . . .
Move me . . .
Fly me . . .
Away and back again
On a moment's notice.

...the only thing we can hope
to do is leave an imprint...

IMPRINTS

The fallen maple leaf,
Having come to moistened rest
On the sidewalk,
Leaves a stencil of itself.
It's red-brown color drained into the
Seemingly hard, porous surface.

It seems to understand
That the only thing we can ever really hope to do
Is to leave an imprint
Of ourselves
On the places we land.

So these questions follow:
What sort of imprints
Do we hope to leave behind us?
And upon what
Or who
Do we hope to leave them?

And what, if in spite of our best intentions,
And dreams,
A wind comes through
And blows us down the sidewalk,
And we affect something
Completely different
From what we ever imagined.

And what if we never know,
Never realize,
All the imprints we have made —
Fleeting or lasting?
And what if we could learn
To let that be
Without our knowing?

So that when we,
Like the leaf,
Blow away
Or crumble to dust,
The imprints we leave
Become our peace.

BOUNDARIES

It is the precious nature
Of clean, clear boundaries
That creates relationship
With intention and integrity.

The smoother, glossy, palpable surface
Of a whole something
Undulates seamlessly with another anything . . .
Everything . . .
Enhancing unique form
And unified existence.

Where one thing ends, so begins another.
Yet a subtle tension remains between the two,
A differentiated connectivity.

Still . . .
Neither have need of self-sacrifice
Or isolation
As a means of individual definition.

The understanding of uniqueness
Depends on the relationship
And the boundary.

Without the ferocious gentleness of boundaries,
Connections become adhesive . . .
Stuck . . .
And all flow,
All momentum,
All individuality,
All potentiality
Is lost.

The Holy runs rampant everywhere...

LAST RESORT?

I can't say what "God" is,
Or isn't.
But I know how to recognize the Holy.
On the tip of the tongue of a friend . . .
Or stranger,
In the slightest touch of a breeze,
Under the silence of snow . . .

On the broad back of a turtle,
In the face of a beggar,
Hanging in the weight of a blackberry branch . . .

Around a bend in the road,
In the flick of a deer's ear,
On the tail of a humming bird . . .

In the sweet dampness of a baby,
The snap-crackle-pop of lightning,
In a moment of synchronicity or inconvenience.

The Holy runs wildly rampant
Everywhere . . .
Untamed,
Unexpected,
Uncontained,
Subtlety abundant,
Lovingly fierce,
And sometimes comical.

Why, on earth,
Would it choose to live in a House of worship?
Confine itself for human-sake?
Stifle its creativity?
Why go inside when you can be everywhere
And everything
All at once?

Perhaps as a last resort
In order to be recognized?

MOMENTARY CROSSING

There are times
    When circumstances are just right . . .
        Like a ripe moon
            A drizzle of rain
                A soupy fog . . .

That a momentary crossing
    From time to timelessness
        Form to formlessness
            Blood and bones to dirt and stones
                Can occur.

When the molecules of me . . .
    The atoms of me . . .
        Forget to be human
            Forget to stay different
                From everything else.

When I am no longer lost
    But discovered
        No longer separate
            But fused into a greater whole
                No longer longing for myself.

RADIANCE

Your radiance needs no translation.
Even though along the way of your life
You may have been taught
To cloak it in acceptability . . .
Make it a safer size . . .
Socially correct it.

When it comes to squelching radiance,
All efforts are futile.
Even if you manage to shroud it completely
It will glow still,
An un-extinguishable ember
Under the temple of your flesh.

You will feel it longing to be seen.
Sense it wanting to be known.
Hunting for a seam in your body,
Tugging at your beliefs,
Fussing with your reasoning and your desire to be safe,
Till it cracks the brittle shell of doubt and mistrust
And spills like honey from your bruised heart.

AMAZING THINGS

Settling into the soft arms of twilight,
I remember . . .
I have seen amazing things today . . .

A wooly bear caterpillar's pilgrimage
To the far, far, far side of the perilous driveway.

A warrior chipmunk,
Perched atop a castle of stones,
Casting curses at the yellow tomcat.

The last dahlia,
Heavy-headed and proud,
Letting go, face up to the sun,
Over the stone wall.

A spider,
Hitchhiking on the wind,
Swinging a thousand spider miles
To the bittersweet vine to set up housekeeping . . .
Again.

A hummingbird,
Not perched, but landed.
A rare moment of still wings
Between blossom battles.

A kindness,
Laid around the shoulders
Of a stranger
Like a colorful shawl.

Yes.
I have seen amazing things today.
And in seeing them — felt them —
I could have missed them,
Had I not been looking for miracles.

What a difference it has made that I noticed them.
What a difference it has made to remember them —
To be grateful for them.
What a difference in how I sleep tonight.
What a difference in how I wake tomorrow.
Want a difference!

DESERT

Even in the most desolate places
Or times,
(Maybe especially there . . . then) . . .
The most surprising,
Most unexpected,
Most welcome vitality appears.

From what seems the least likely possibility
Some striking color emerges.
Some original scent,
Some rhythmic sound.
A rustle . . .
A flutter . . .
Something dormant waking up.

In loneliness, company.
In separateness, synergy.
In thirst, oasis.
In hunger, feast.
In heat, shade.
In death, life.

Like a dessert,
Life waits inside . . .
Beside . . .
Underneath
Whatever seems endless,
Unbearable,
Or forsaken,
(Maybe especially there . . . then . . .) . . .
Then swings from "Now" to "Next"
And tilts my perspective
Again and again.

— Joshua Tree National Park, 2013

BALSAM BRANCH INTERLUDE

Two dark eyes watching
From beneath the balsam branch.

Two distant eyes gazing straight ahead,
down the path,
unaware . . .

Two velvet ears
Twitching in silent instinctive hesitation.
Two spiral ears with headphones
Tuning out the noise of the day.

One white tail
Poised perfectly still in single-pointed focus.
One tail-forgotten pair of hips
Churning in directed rhythm.

Two hearts beating hard and fast.
One from curiosity close to fear.
The other with heated purpose yet unclear.

One being, ready to run.
The other, running to be ready.

BEACH TRANSITION

Given the opportunity,
A beach can stop me in my tracks,
The magnetism of salt water
Inescapable.
The distinct possibility of a cleansing baptism
Seeming likely in the exhale of waves that
Deepens my own breath,
Lowers my own ribs,
Softens my spine,
Blurs my questions
And empties what was almost too full.

The enzymes in bone calcium sand
Become an instant catalyst
That distance me from responsibilities.
Sun-soothing, watery breezes quench some forgotten thirst
And satiate something inside
That has gone hungry for too long.

Then I begin to "get" the joke
That the gulls have thought hilarious all along.
Intoxicated by the incense of saline
And sunscreen,
The punch lines become discernable.
And I remember to be giddy
To the point that some younger me
Wakes up and cancels any plans to leave
Having forgotten
That any other way of life
Exists.

THE ONLY
IMPORTANT THING . . .

She had become the age at which
Old friends and acquaintances
Would stop now and then
To ask each other,
"Is she still alive?"

This came as a surprise to her,
And,
Once accepted,
Informed the way she approached her days.

She instantly understood the waste of regret,
The worthlessness of "what ifs,"
The ridiculousness of waiting . . .

The delight of spontaneity.

And the blessed power
Of finally living
In each present moment
Became the only important thing.

And honeybees view me as
no larger... or smaller...
than a wing
    and a prayer.

FALLEN

I have fallen off the edge of my ego . . .
    Again . . .
        Into a strange garden
            Of curious uncertainty.

The landing was somewhat softer . . .
    This time . . .
        Having tumbled into a warm nest
            Thickly feathered by the memories
                Of previous descents.

It's more familiar down here . . .
    Now . . .
        Though still painful.
            You see, it's time to fledge —
                Time to kick myself out of the safety nest,
                    Over the edge . . .

To stand amid the ego-less things
Where there is no need to fight . . . or fly . . . or freeze.

Where snapdragons giggle
At my futile attempts to run the world.
And honeybees view me as no larger . . . or smaller . . .
Than a wing and a prayer.

Where sunflowers shake their heads
At my hurtful discretions,

And the morning glory vines tug and pull
My self-forgiveness to the surface
So the breath of butterflies can blow me apart,
And the mud wasps can patch my self-worth.

THE RISING

There is a seam in time
At dusk,
During which you can sense
The long, slow, relaxed exhale
Of the sun
As he sets;
His glow fading
Down and down . . .
Lost behind the turning of the day.

Then,
In the fleeting moments
Just before the moon rises up
Over her mountain,
A sweet stillness
At the end of that big exhale.
Not a holding of breath,
But a pause . . .
A felt sense of transition,
Especially if crickets are singing,
Or a light breeze is shifting,
Or a soft snow is falling,
Or your heart is searching.

A pause in which you can hear
The silence behind sounds,
And something reaches into your soul
And spreads a balm
Over your aches and questions,
And the cooling moon shows you
That it is never really necessary
To "take" a breath,
Rather simply receive your next big inhale,
Making your own rising possible
Again . . . and again.

THE YEAR

How impressively short a year can be,
Once thought long,
Or even hard.
How full.
How rich.
How abundant,
Significant, exhausting, extraordinary.
A marathon of moments.
An anthology of experiences.
A treasury of memories
Of dreams come true,
Of heart-testing challenges,
Of manifested visions,
Of profound loss,
Of new endeavors,
Of unexpected turns,
Of brave adventures
And realized fears,
Of resounding joy
And dismantling grief,
Of pregnant bellies
And empty rooms.
Has it really been just 12 months?
Let me sit down right here,
By the trail of the year,
And rest — just for today.
I'll reflect on my questions and answers,
Doubts and hopes,
Loves and fears.
Then I'll pick myself up,
Tighten my bootlaces,
And,
Just like time,
I'll begin again.

KIND-HEARTED
GREAT MYSTERY

Kind-Hearted Great Mystery,
I do not forget you.
I do not abandon you,
Even though I am a Human Being,
And stumble everyday
And almost forget.

Today I want to remember.
I want to feel your great fingers
Dip into my heart
And tug at my very fascia
Until my whole body
Realigns with Grace . . .
Until I once again understand
That absolutely everything —
Everything —
Has a reason for being,
A purpose,
A place and a time.

I want to hear your song again,
Feel your breath again,
See your face again . . .
Until my pain —
Again —
Becomes my teacher,
My grief becomes my beauty,
My joy becomes my way of life.

ABOUT THE AUTHOR

Elissa Cobb has been practicing yoga and meditation for more than 35 years. She is currently co-owner of Yarn & Yoga, a yarn shop and yoga studio in her hometown of Bristol, Vermont. Her first book, *The Forgotten Body: A Way of Knowing and Understanding Self*, was published in 2008 by Satya House Publications and was a ForeWord Book of the Year finalist. You can contact Elissa at www.elissacobb.com.

CPSIA information can be obtained
at www.ICGtesting.com
Printed in the USA
BVOW10s2039241016
465907BV00004B/4/P